THE WARFARE OF A *Woman*

APOSTOLIC INSTRUCTIONS FOR *Victory*

APOSTLE LIZELLE BRADLEY

Hov PUBLISHING

THE WARFARE OF A *Woman*
APOSTOLIC INSTRUCTIONS FOR *VICTORY*

Copyright ©2019 by Lizelle Bradley

All rights reserved. No part of this book may be reproduced, copied, stored or transmitted in any form or by any means – graphic, electronic, or mechanical, including photocopying, recording, or information storage and retrieval systems without the prior written permission of Lizelle Bradley or HOV Publishing except where permitted by law.

Scriptures taken from the King James Version. Copyright ©1991 by World Bible Publishers, Inc. Used by permission. All rights reserved.

HOV Publishing a division of HOV, LLC.
www.hopeofvisionpublishing.com
hopeofvision@gmail.com

Covenant Connection Publishing

Cover Design: HOV Design Solutions
Editor: Amy Owens for Clarity Communication
Proofreader: Dianna Knox-Cooper

Write the Author Apostle Lizelle Bradley at:
Email: Bradleylizelle@gmail.com

For more information about special discounts for bulk purchases, please contact: Bradleylizelle@gmail.com.

ISBN 978-1-942871-53-8

Library of Congress Control Number: 2019932657

10 9 8 7 6 5 4 3 2 1

Printed in the United States of America

OPENING PRAYER

Most Gracious and Heavenly Father, I come boldly before your Throne of Grace. I come asking you to prepare my readers to expect an extraordinary shift in their spirits as they begin to encounter the apostolic anointing that rests on these pages! My prayer is that each nugget, each revelation, and each solution given will bring about a change in someone's life.

In Jesus' name, Amen.

ENDORSEMENTS

Every Christian is periodically susceptible to challenges and frustrations that appear to be preternatural in origin. In The Warfare of a Woman, Apostle Lizelle Bradley gives pragmatic, systematic strategies for realizing victory in countless situations. Her first-hand experiences as a woman in business and a woman on the frontlines of ministry have postured her to have a valid voice in encouraging readers to overcome opposition by walking according to God's Word. This instructional tool of wisdom is a must-read for every Christian.

Sharon Y. Riley, Senior Pastor
Agape Perfecting Praise & Worship Center,
Orlando, FL

As we struggle in this life that we have been presented with, while reading Apostle Lizelle Bradley's book, The Warfare of a Woman, I was captivated by the anointing that flowed. This book represents everything that we need as Christians to give us guidance and direction while dealing with the tactics of the enemy.

This book is an eye-opener for you to focus on God's intent for your life and to embrace the uniqueness for the purpose He has established for you as a Christian, to know how to fight the good fight of faith, and handle warfare properly through the guidance of the word of God.

The author relates this book in a way that will captivate you and help to reprogram, remove self-destructive behaviors, and most of all deal with the battle of the mind through scripture.

This is a very powerful and practical book that will give you strength. There is a message that will conform and transform your very life. This book will guide and direct you into a greater understanding concerning warfare and the limitless armor that God has equipped us with to annihilate the enemy out of every area of our lives.

Apostle Sherol D. Larkin
335 W. Central Ave.
Lake Wales, Fl. 33853
(863) 679-6000

In this crazy, cruel world, women have always been attacked with some form of warfare. Therefore, it is imperative that we keep in mind and rest assured that God's word is true, for II Corinthians 10:4 reminds us that "The weapons of our warfare are not carnal, but mighty through God to the pulling down of strongholds."

The word warfare comes from the Greek word strateia (strategy) which means military service. Figuratively speaking, warfare means the apostolic career—as one of hardship and danger.
Women must understand that warfare is more spiritual than natural. From the beginning, the enemy waged warfare against the woman when she was beguiled in the garden. Nevertheless, God had a strategy. His strategy was that there was a lamb slain before the foundation of the world and a promise given that the seed of the woman would crush the head of the seed of the enemy.

The strategic plan was fulfilled in time which brought about a great victory. Likewise, God wants to bring victory to your life by apostolically aligning you with His strategy and instructions. Apostle Bradley provides meticulous instructions on how God wants to use women to be an effective representation of what He wants to do in His kingdom and the world.

Every woman needs a strategy, and this book will provide women with the strategy that is needed to be fortified and well prepared in a world that presents continuous challenges.

Apostle Jarvis Marshall
Spirit life Ministry, Auburndale Fl.

"Lizelle Bradley has written a must-read for anyone needing insight to the Warfare of a Woman...Read this book - and learn from one of God's greatest generals."

Elder Anthony J. Brown, Senior Pastor
Macedonia Primitive Baptist Church

"I encourage you to read this book with an open heart full of obedience to the Lord Jesus Christ. We often acknowledge the warfare but lack the instructions to Victory. Hear, and refuse it not. May the Lord bless you as you take heed to His instructions. Victory is yours!"

Proverbs 8:33, *Hear instruction and be wise and refuse it not.*

Dr. Monique Harris,
Apostle of Jesus Is Lord Ministry Inc.

When it comes to spiritual warfare Apostle Bradley is one of the best teachers. Her experience, knowledge and anointing surpassing that of years or time. I'm positive this book will teach you to recognize all plots and attacks. It is designed to give you a new perceptive and lead you into your wealthy place- victory. I am proud to say that one of God's generals has once again heard from heaven.

I love that Apostle confronts shame and teaches the reader to overcome. She reestablishes the worth of the woman and teaches her to value her God-given authority. As you read this book you will become enlighten to God's thoughts about you, his love for you and his grace that is upon you! Apostle Bradley is one of heavens best!

J.D. Bellamy

DEDICATION

I proudly, with much respect, dedicate this book to a young lady who truly saw the natural side of my warfare first hand, as a young girl in school. She always was a person of few words through it all and was always there to do whatever I needed her to do. I was in a very abusive relationship at one time in my life, and I allowed someone to TAKE MY VOICE. My allowing that caused the people connected to me to feel the same unexplainable pain and she was one of them.

So, with much appreciation I dedicate my book, *The Warfare of a Woman* to my daughter Keke, "Pastor A." Through all of what she saw me go through, she NEVER asked a question, commented, or said one word. I could see the hurt that she felt for me in her eyes, but she never got involved. She was there when her niece, my first granddaughter was born and she missed days of school to help me with her because she knew my heart. She wasn't happy about it, but I knew in my heart that she did it just for me. She finally graduated from school, and moved away, to start her own life. God intervened and sent her right back to work in the ministry with me.

    I truly believe God allowed her to see a lot in my life so that she would understand my journey. I'm very proud of her walk with God and she is currently in training as the successor of our ministry, Winning Souls For The Kingdom International. She is truly a woman of God, with no compromise, when it comes to His word, and most of all, she is still that little girl that looks out for her MOM. I think she believes she's my mom.

ACKNOWLEDGEMENTS

I believe that we are the product of pioneers who have passed through our lives at some point of time. I could never in one book, begin to acknowledge all the generals, and vehicles of Wisdom who have poured into me, but I want to acknowledge a few of them that God allowed to pass through my life.

First and foremost, I want to acknowledge, Pastor Sharon Y. Riley of Agape Perfecting Praise & Worship Center in Orlando, Florida. In 2001, as newlyweds, my husband (Bishop Jeffery K, Bradley) and I moved to Orlando to begin our new life. We both knew that going to church was not optional. One day I was at the neighborhood laundry as I noticed a church that sat behind the laundry. I shared it with my husband and we went to the service that Sunday. It was amazing; I had never in my life seen deliverance preached with so much passion and authority. God spoke to me immediately in that service and said, "Stay put; this is your training ground." I confess that was the first time I knew without a doubt that the voice I heard was God. We obeyed and stayed under her leadership for 5 years.

Pastor Riley, encouraged me so much just through the word of God. I literally fell in love with God just through the word. Even though we were strangers, Pastor Riley never treated us any different. We went to every service, paid tithes and offerings, and sowed seeds like we belonged there. Pastor Riley always rightly divided the word of God, with no compromise. I learned through her to just say what God said and let the chips fall where they fall. Pastor Riley helped my husband sharpen his gift of evangelism outreach. I watched Pastor Riley, touch so many lives through outreach; she would always demonstrate how Jesus went out and touched the lost. I adopted a great passion for the homeless through what I saw her do and she never tried to make a platform for herself or be noticed; she always taught. Your gift will make room for you, I thank God so much for this awesome Woman of God and the things she demonstrated through her life. she has always stood out to me as being holy with no compromise. Thank you so much Pastor Sharon Y. Riley.

I would like to acknowledge a Woman of God who was the first one that heard the word of the Lord concerning me writing a book over 10 years ago, Prophetess Michon Chunn Garrett. She has been the one pushing me to share the warfare that I survived publicly and privately. For years she would always say, "You don't have to write, I can be your ghost writer." I would always brush her off.

She has prophesied over my life in so many areas, and all has come to pass, just like this book has. Prophetess Michon has been an inspiration in my life. Even while serving as my Armor Bearer, she never stops saying to me whatever the Lord had spoken concerning my life. *The Warfare of A Woman*, from the spiritual aspect was truly birthed before her very eyes, so I honor her for not allowing her submission to me as her leader to stop her from releasing God's word over my life.

I want to truly acknowledge my husband, Bishop Jeffery Bradley, and my children for bearing the years of ministry, that many times called for me to be away from home for long hours, and sometimes days. My husband has been nothing but Great! When it comes to the work that God has called me to in ministry, I love and appreciate him for covering me. My husband has allowed and trusted me to minister not only to women but men as well. He is truly the piece that completes my puzzle.

TABLE OF CONTENTS

FOREWORD xvii

INTRODUCTION ....……….. xx

CHAPTER 1 1
Her Emotional Warfare

CHAPTER 2 7
Her Shameful Warfare

CHAPTER 3 13
Unnecessary Warfare

CHAPTER 4 20
Her Silent Warfare

CHAPTER 5 28
Her Warfare of Regret

CHAPTER 6 34
The Warfare of Her Rejection

CHAPTER 7 40
The Warfare of Her Ministry

CHAPTER 8 45
The Warfare of Her Family

CHAPTER 9 50
The Warfare of Her Faith

CHAPTER 10 56
The Warfare of Her Deliverance

AFTERWORD..62

JOURNAL 69

FOREWORD

It is not often in life that a woman can read a book chapter by chapter, line by line, that pulls the covers from a mirrored façade cloaked with the deception of a self-made image of perfection. She is blinded by ignorance to the warfare that lies within her gates and knocks at her heart, mind, and soul to become a silly woman—a prey for the predator, and a casualty of war. There is no need to be a silly woman; you can become an empowered woman. Women of God, this book, *The Warfare of A Woman*, will reveal your battles and give you the weapons to destroy the forces that hold you fast to the past.

The *Warfare of A Woman* is a severe struggle and must be won and maintained. The Apostolic Instructions of Victory in this awesome book, if applied, allows a woman the spiritual freedom to become all that God has predestined her to be. The conflicts of war can be perpetual because of the lack of knowledge when choosing your battles and being careful not to entrap ourselves with contentment. The voice of God has spoken openly to Apostle Lizelle Bradley upon the pages in this book to bring deliverance to His daughters.

Understand that the struggle can be overwhelming to you without the knowledge of your combatants. However, it does not matter your age or the length of time you have been in the Body of Christ; all are vulnerable to warfare with our enemy. The knowledge released in this book is priceless for it reveals the truth that you can win the war!

The Apostle has opened my eyes to the warfare that was still raging in my life and holding me fast to my past. Yes, The Warfare of Rejection bound me in my mind, emotions, lessened my ability to trust, and kept me from seeing totally that my Father has never rejected me; nor has He rejected you.

---

*"Rejection can change the way you see and respond to life." ~**Apostle Lizelle Bradley***

God is using Apostle Lizelle Bradley to break the chains of ignorance concerning *The Warfare of A Woman*. With these Apostolic Instructions, she is empowering women to equip themselves with weapons of war to identify and defeat the warfare of shame, regret, faith, ministry, deliverance, silent, emotional, rejection, family, and the unnecessary warfare. Apostle Bradley has written this book for such a time as this, for Joel declared that God's daughters and handmaidens should RISE and SOAR for this is our time!

Apostle, I am anxiously waiting for the sequel and the next Apostolic Word of Instructions that will bring change, empowerment, and a Revolutionary Revival to the hearts of our Father's Daughters!

Apostle Juanita Clay, Embrace Logistic Inc., Henderson, TN

INTRODUCTION

You have in your hands not just a book, but 10 chapters of apostolic strategies that have been presented through the Holy Ghost which I believe God has mandated that I write, so you can pick it up on a daily basis, and deal with daily warfare. I desire that you would keep it on hand and read it over and over again to get it in your spirit, so that you would not be overwhelmed with warfare.

This I know for a fact, this is the time for *The Warfare of a Woman* to be released because after years of prophecy spoken over my life, I still didn't move to write. It wasn't that I didn't believe the prophecies, it was that I refused to be another leader or Pastor who *needed* to be an author to add the word to my Bio. I have always said to myself, "If I step into anything, first it has to be God, second I want to be an Impact, not an Impression. The principles and instructions in this book are those that I personally experienced, and some I have seen others experience firsthand.

I write this book with much compassion for my readers, because many of you have never been taught true warfare, especially us as women. We have been taught how to operate in emotions, and not deal with the warfare, or confront our issues.

The Spirit of the Lord has assigned me to document revelation and apostolic strategies and make them available to women seeking these strategies to overcome this thing called Warfare!

I write this book so that women can recognize and identify where their warfare comes from and how to minimize warfare not only through the Word of God, but also through self-evaluation and embracing true deliverance in themselves when God reveals it. In this Introduction, I want to make it clear that my readers understand that in order to fully have victory in your warfare, it's going to take:

1. A made-up mind;
2. Embracing and applying these strategies;
3. A relationship with God.

As an Apostle, I'm pretty sure if any Apostles are reading this book, they would agree that they have dealt with warfare on a whole different level since properly embracing their calling as an Apostle.

I write this book with much experience so that my life is transparent on each page, in some form or fashion. My testimony is far beyond a 10-chapter book, but I believe the little that I have shared in this book will help women all over to know that warfare is not the end of the world and that it can be WON!

I write this book as one who has definitely learned through the principles and strategies that I have outlined in this book, and I have won many battles by obeying God's instructions. One of my most favorite instructions that came from God through warfare was when God told me, "W*hen you're right, you don't fight."* Some were easy, and some weren't, but I learned that life deals us hands that we MUST play by His book.

I write this book to help women understand their DNA, which is about 90% Emotion! Some of us say, that we are not emotional. I did too, but let me help a sista' out; there are many kinds of emotions:

1. Those that can be maintained;
2. Those that get out of control;
3. Those that we just ignore; and
4. Those that belong to others, but we chose to carry them ourselves

I write this book to help women rightly divide these emotions, and aim to hit the target, so that victory can be yours.

I write this book after so many years of seeing myself and other women trapped in situations that their emotions had a tight grip on, causing them to be entangled in relationships, jobs, ministries, and friendships, etc. that they shouldn't have been in.

I write this book not to bring my readers back to their past, but to rightly divide the word of God, through the scriptures referenced in each chapter so that clarity can be attained on how to deal with spiritual warfare.

Apostle Lizelle Bradley

"A woman's heart should be so hidden in God that a man has to seek Him just to find her."
~Max Lucado

CHAPTER 1

Her Emotional Warfare

"Our feelings are unreliable and cannot be trusted to convey truth." ~Joyce Meyer

---

A happy heart is good medicine and a cheerful mind works healing, but a broken spirit dries up the bones. ~Proverbs 17:22

"The sooner we learn feelings are fickle, the better off we are." ~Joyce Meyer

When it comes to the Christian life, we are either winning or losing. But we are all involved in a battle. In this chapter, I want to look at the warfare a woman faces in her emotions.

Warfare: a struggle between two enemies

---

*The Believer's life is not a playground, but a battleground. ~**Apostle Lizelle Bradley***

Her Emotional Warfare

Genesis 25 covers a very interesting story from the life of Isaac and his wife, Rebekah. Isaac entreated the Lord because Rebekah was barren; The Lord heard and answered Isaac's prayers and Rebekah conceived.

Yet, there was *Warfare in her Womb!* The warfare was because she had two different nations in her. We know them as Jacob and Esau and they literally warred inside her womb.

As I looked at this passage, the Lord began to reveal to me, just like Rebekah, most women have a war going on inside of them; an emotional war.

Although we may not have two different *nations* warring within us, we do have two opposing natures at war.

Examples of our two natures are:

- Flesh and Spirit
- Right and Wrong
- Good and Evil
- God's Will and the Enemy's Will

These two different natures have their own agendas and in order to fulfill their agendas, they come after our emotions. I really want you to understand that our emotions are neutral and can be used by either our flesh or spirit, right or wrong, or good or evil. Our emotions can give energy either to God's will for our lives or the will of the enemy.

This creates the war because the enemy knows that we are already emotional creatures and he tries to use our emotions to accomplish his agenda.

Apostle Paul's words regarding this are found in Romans 7:21-23.

This is warfare, saints! The desire to do good, though I being present. In Romans 7:23, the Apostle Paul shares that he found himself in captivity held by the law of sin.

Women, this is why we must win the war that's going on in our wombs; when we are taken captive, we then serve the law of sin and disobedience. This is how the enemy distracts, divides, defeats, and destroys.

- The enemy **distracts** us through **deception**;
- The enemy **divides** us through **disputes**;
- The enemy **defeats** us through **discord**; and
- The enemy **destroys** us through **disobedience**.

The goal of the enemy is to get us to birth the wrong agendas.

"You must win the battle before you give birth."
~Apostle Lizelle Bradley

So many women are giving birth to visions, assignments, and agendas that God has nothing to do with simply because they didn't win the battle before they gave birth. Look at all of the ministries that were birthed because somebody lost the battle in their womb. Instead of handling offense, rebuke, or a disagreement according to the word of God, they allowed the enemy to attach his agenda to their emotions and they birthed something God didn't ordain. I think about the marriages that ended in divorce because someone allowed the enemy to gain access to their emotions.

The battle on the inside of you is so much bigger than you! ~Apostle Lizelle Bradley

---

The enemy wants to destroy everything that God has called you to do. Women, this is why whenever we operate in our emotions, we put everything that God has entrusted into our care in harm's way. This can include our marriages, families, ministries, friendships, business deals, and opportunities.

When we operate in our emotions, we do not process things biblically, so we start to move out of sync with God.

*"Our successes and failures actually depend on our emotional situation." ~**Apostle Lizelle Bradley***

Even in my marriage whenever my husband and I have *heated fellowships* there are times that we both have to relinquish our views; we both have to look to God's Word for direction.

Understand that men are *positional* while women are *emotional*. God set the man as the head (which is positional). When we look at the men who experienced defeat in the Bible, they were the ones who moved out of the *place* that God ordained for them to be. Even now, men are defeated when they move from the *place* God ordained.

Women in the Bible, and even today, experience defeat when we allow our *emotions to make decisions for us.*

When the enemy wants to take us off course, he will always attack our emotions, but we must take ACTION against the attack launched at our emotions. What do I mean by *take ACTION*?

A...*Acknowledge* your emotions;
C...*Consider* why you have then;
T...*Take* authority over them;
I...*Identify* a Biblical response to them;
O...*Obey* the Holy Spirit's leading; and
N...*Nurture* your Spirit

CHAPTER 2

Her Shameful Warfare

"You must learn, you must let God teach you, that the only way to get rid of your past is to make a future out of it. God will waste nothing."
~Phillips Brooks

As you wait for the revealing of our Lord Jesus Christ, who will sustain you to the end, guiltless in the day of our Lord Jesus Christ. God is faithful, by whom you were called into the fellowship of his Son, Jesus Christ our Lord. ~1 Corinthians 1:7-9

"Failing is not a disgrace unless you make it the last chapter of your book." ~Jack Hyles

Shame is a very strong emotion that can convince us that we are flawed or unworthy. It shuts down, inhibits, and separates us from others. Shame is so personal! It's a painful feeling of humiliation that we've done something wrong or that there's something disgraceful or embarrassing about us.

It's the secret emotion that can sit in us like a poison and the last thing we want to do is bring it out in the open.

As women, most of our shame stems from our youth and we carry the shame from things we literally had no control over. Because we lacked an outlet and so many of us have never been delivered, we live out our days in shame.

It was all we had!

Growing up with 14 siblings, it was hard to feel special or spoiled because everything was basically shared. My mother was a single mom raising a house filled with kids; we never lived lavishly but we all knew that we were loved. I remember clearly wearing *hand-me-downs;* for those who are not familiar with hand-me-downs, they are clothes handed down from your older siblings.

Going to school was tough because I felt as if I was less than those who lived lives that I considered privileged. I was even afraid to affiliate with certain groups in school for fear that they would make fun of me; over time those feelings began to produce shame.

While you're reading this book, perhaps you have thought of the things that opened the door to shame in your life. Some of you were just like me and you had to live with not enough. However, others have had to deal with verbal abuse, sexual abuse, physical abuse, substance abuse, or feelings of inadequacy; because of your experiences you now live in shame.

In the Bible, 2 Samuel Chapter 13 covers the story of Amnon and Tamar, and it reveals how the spirit of shame can be released into you through the actions of another. Her own brother took advantage of her and raped her, sending her away in shame.

It's one thing to be taken advantage of; it's another story when the person who has taken advantage of you dismisses you causing you to make sense out of your *new* reality. How many have been dismissed by someone who violated you and planted the seed of shame in you? Even today you still deal with the effect of the shame of your youth.

Her Shameful Warfare

Where Do I Go from Here?

You will be surprised of those who had nowhere to turn and so they began to live inaccurate renditions of who they were supposed to be.

- **Many** start to abuse others out of the anger of being abused.
- **Many** turn to an alternative lifestyle because of the abuse imposed on them.
- **Many** begin to abuse substance (drugs, alcohol);
- **Many** become addicted to pornography because their sexual appetites are all over the place.

Then there are those who, unlike Tamar, had to deal with uninvited shame. There are those who are directly responsible for their shame. We don't like to talk about it but sometimes we can play a major role in the shame we exist in.

Esther 1 covers the story of Vashti who had an amazing life. She lived in the palace but she became common with the King. And when the king made a request of her, she denied him. This text tells us that Vashti refused the King.

Wow! That sounds like so many of us who are in a privileged position that we take for granted, and then we find ourselves rejecting the King.

Many wanted to know what would happen to Vashti as a result of her disobedience. If it ever got out that Vashti dishonored the King, every king would have a problem on their hands, so Vashti was dismissed in shame and she lived the rest of her life under shame's umbrella.

Ladies, sometimes when we fail to operate in wisdom, we mismanage an opportunity that the Lord has set in our paths. Everything working against us is not *always* the devil; sometimes we lack wisdom, humility, and honor and because of that we end up opening the door to a life of shame.

You can be delivered!

If you will get victory over shame and turn your depression into a dream; mistakes into ministry; and bondage into your greatest breakthrough, you must:

- Renew your relationship with God
- Forgive yourself and those who trespass against you
- Be real about your struggle with shame
- Employ scriptural solutions

Understand this, even though it's the goal of the enemy that you die in shame, because of your covenant with Jesus Christ an anointing to outlive shame now rests on your life. In Jesus' name, I command you to walk in total victory over the spirit of shame.

Our stories are not meant for everyone. Hearing them is a privilege, and we should always ask ourselves this question before we share: *"Who has earned the right to hear my story?"* If we have one or two people in our lives who can sit with us and hold space for our shame stories, and love us for our strengths and struggles, we are incredibly lucky. If we have a friend, or small group of friends, or family who embraces our imperfections, vulnerabilities, and power, and fills us with a sense of belonging, we are incredibly lucky.

~**Brene Brown**

CHAPTER 3

Unnecessary Warfare

"Peace is not absence of conflict, it is the ability to handle conflict by peaceful means."
~Ronald Reagan

"Conflict cannot survive without your participation." ~Wayne Dyer

---

"Whenever you're in conflict with someone, there is one factor that can make the difference between damaging your relationship and deepening it. That factor is attitude." ~William James

There are certain challenges and problems we face in life that simply go with the journey. Especially when you are a believer the Bible tells us, in 2 Timothy 3:12 that "Yea, and all that will live godly in Christ Jesus shall suffer persecution."

We must expect some challenges because of our commitment to Jesus Christ, however women, I'm sure like myself you've had your share of warfare that could have been avoided. So many are faced with conflicts in life, marriage, friendships, business, and even ministry that they lacked the wisdom to prevent.

As I was praying, I began to think about how so many are dealing with unnecessary warfare in so many areas, mostly because of the demons of disobedience and discontentment.

Disobedience is defined as failure or refusal to obey rules or someone in authority.

Wow! There's so much revelation in that definition. What many are experiencing today actually reflects an act of disobedience and the refusal in most cases to obey God, the Word of God, or an authority in their life.

---

*"Disobedience will give birth to unnecessary warfare." ~**Apostle Lizelle Bradley***

Consider Gehazi, the servant of Elisha. Gehazi was in a privileged position as the servant of one of the most powerful prophets of his day. However, because of his refusal to stay aligned with the will of God he found himself operating in a spirit of greed that would affect generations to come.

"Our decisions will affect those we are connected to." ~Apostle Lizelle Bradley

Gehazi went behind the Prophet Elisha's back because he saw an opportunity to profit. Understand that Gehazi's greed deprived him of future blessings. After negotiating with Naaman, Gehazi received from him things that neither God, nor the Prophet had authorized. The Prophet called him to a place of accountability and judgement.

In 2 Kings 5:26-27, we read: But Elisha said to him, "Was not my spirit with you when the man got down from his chariot to meet you? Is this the time to take money or to accept clothes—or olive groves and vineyards, or flocks and herds, or male and female slaves? Naaman's leprosy will cling to you and to your descendants forever." Then Gehazi went from Elisha's presence and his skin was leprous—it had become as white as snow.

Wow! Gehazi's disobedience and greed caused him to miss out on his destiny and not only

Unnecessary Warfare

was he afflicted leprosy, but the Prophet told him that his descendants would forever be afflicted.

It is safe for me to say that this was not the will of God for Gehazi; this was self-inflicted and simply Unnecessary Warfare—warfare birthed out of disobedience and greed.

"Don't allow disobedience to change the destiny that God has ordained for your life."
~Apostle Lizelle Bradley

Discontentment is another demon that will open the door to Unnecessary Warfare. Here's why: In Hebrews 12:5b, the Bible says, *"Be content with what you have."* This is because we can find ourselves moving away from God's will because of discontentment.

Discontentment is defined as a restless desire or craving for something one does not have.

2 Samuel 11 covers the story of David's discontentment. He was the king and although he literally had any and everything he desired, he wanted more.

We must guard ourselves against this spirit because this is the root cause why so many marriages, ministries, and people in general are going through Unnecessary Warfare. God has given you everything you need but you still want more.

2 Samuel 11:2-5 tells us, "One evening David got up from his bed and walked around on the roof of the palace. From the roof he saw a woman bathing. The woman was very beautiful, and David sent someone to find out about her. The man said, 'She is Bathsheba, the daughter of Eliam and the wife of Uriah the Hittite.' Then David sent messengers to get her. She came to him, and he slept with her. (Now she was purifying herself from her monthly uncleanness.) Then she went back home. The woman conceived and sent word to David, saying, "I am pregnant."

David's discontentment created a dilemma that cost him almost everything.

Whenever we are driven by discontentment, we fail to calculate the price that must be paid because of our dissatisfaction. David had to cover his sinful decision and this led him into a direction that caused Bathsheba to deal with Unnecessary Warfare as well. This is why as leaders with influence, we cannot mismanage our influence because others will end up living out the penalty of our disobedience and discontentment.

In 2 Samuel 11:14-15, we read that, "In the morning David wrote a letter to Joab and sent it with Uriah. *15* In it he wrote, "Put Uriah out in front where the fighting is fiercest. Then withdraw from him so he will be struck down and die."

Wow, David was dealing with matters that God never ordained. Because not only had Bathsheba lost her covering (husband) but even the child born would die because of David's disobedience and discontentment.

In 2 Samuel 12:14 we continue to read, "However, because by this deed you have given great occasion to the enemies of the Lord to blaspheme, the child also *who is* born to you shall surely die."

Do you see this? Everything connected to David went through Unnecessary Warfare because of him. This is why we must seek the face of God like never before for true deliverance; Unnecessary Warfare is the harvest of disobedience and discontentment. Guard yourself in this hour against environments and influences that will open the gate to Unnecessary Warfare because the enemy will use Unnecessary Warfare to destroy what God has called you to accomplish on the earth. Further, what's even sadder is that innocent people will suffer because *you* didn't want to be delivered.

I pray that after reading this chapter, you will check yourself and see if disobedience or discontentment is abiding in you. I command you to call yourself to accountability. Do not allow these spirits to open the gate to Unnecessary Warfare. You can be delivered now!

CHAPTER 4

Her Silent Warfare

Everything may not be perfect. There are things that may need to change, but you have the grace to be happy today. ~Joel Osteen

---

Our lives begin to end the day we become silent about things that matter.
~Martin Luther King Jr.

It doesn't take much effort to do what everyone else is doing. A dead fish can float downstream; it takes a live one to swim upstream. It's easy to be common. The pressure comes when you decide to be uncommon. ~Joel Osteen

Her Silent Warfare

1 Samuel 25:3-17

3 Now the name of the man was Nabal; and the name of his wife Abigail: and she was a woman of good understanding, and of a beautiful countenance: but the man was churlish and evil in his doings; and he was of the house of Caleb.
4 And David heard in the wilderness that Nabal did shear his sheep.
5 And David sent out ten young men, and David said unto the young men, Get you up to Carmel, and go to Nabal, and greet him in my name:
6 And thus shall ye say to him that liveth in prosperity, Peace be both to thee, and peace be to thine house, and peace be unto all that thou hast.
7 And now I have heard that thou hast shearers: now thy shepherds which were with us, we hurt them not, neither was there ought missing unto them, all the while they were in Carmel.
8 Ask thy young men, and they will shew thee. Wherefore let the young men find favour in thine eyes: for we come in a good day: give, I pray thee, whatsoever cometh to thine hand unto thy servants, and to thy son David.
9 And when David's young men came, they spake to Nabal according to all those words in the name of David, and ceased.
10 And Nabal answered David's servants, and said, Who is David? and who is the son of Jesse? there be many servants now a days that break away every man from his master.

11 Shall I then take my bread, and my water, and my flesh that I have killed for my shearers, and give it unto men, whom I know not whence they be?
12 So David's young men turned their way, and went again, and came and told him all those sayings.
13 And David said unto his men, Gird ye on every man his sword. And they girded on every man his sword; and David also girded on his sword: and there went up after David about four hundred men; and two hundred abode by the stuff.
14 But one of the young men told Abigail, Nabal's wife, saying, Behold, David sent messengers out of the wilderness to salute our master; and he railed on them.
15 But the men were very good unto us, and we were not hurt, neither missed we any thing, as long as we were conversant with them, when we were in the fields:
16 They were a wall unto us both by night and day, all the while we were with them keeping the sheep.
17 Now therefore know and consider what thou wilt do; for evil is determined against our master, and against all his household: for he is such a son of Belial, that a man cannot speak to him.

I've shared in previous chapters how this book was birthed out of personal experiences, some direct and others indirect. That's because a part of my ministry is to mentor women. This portion of my ministry gives me access into the many different complexions of warfare that women that deal with. I'm amazed at the revelations God gives me while I'm talking to or praying for another woman. There have been times when I was preaching and I would discern the warfare in the room. This is because the anointing on my life allows me to usher women dealing with warfare into their place of deliverance.

There's nothing more disturbing to me than seeing a woman lose the battle. I say that because many are being defeated and some have been defeated and don't even know it.

Your victory is in your voice!
~Apostle Lizelle Bradley

In 1 Samuel 25, we learn of a very powerful woman in Bible named Abigail. With her voice, Abigail brought victory to her entire family. My mother would tell us often, "Some things are best kept silent." What she was saying was you must operate in wisdom if you're going to speak. There are those who talk just to be talking and they really don't understand the power of their voice.

Knowing when to speak is just as important as what you say! *~Apostle Lizelle Bradley*

Although Abigail refused to let silence define her, you'll be surprised by those who have lost their voice. Many women have been constantly told that their opinion doesn't matter, that they have no say in a matter, or they are simply not being heard; when women feel that their voice is taken for granted, they move into a mode of silence. We want to be heard; by nature, women are communicators so they find themselves living life on mute.

Silence is defined as not to speak

God knows the value of your voice so there are times when He will set up circumstances just to get you to say something. Abigail was married to a very controlling man by the name of Nabal. Nabal was so demanding that it caused Abigail's voice to become unnecessary. So many women have allowed a marriage, relationship, and even a ministry to take their voice. They start to feel like their words are worthless. This is the plan of the enemy because if they lose their voice, they'll lose their victory.

God permitted Abigail to be in a position where she could no longer be silent. I hear this in my spirit for you while you're reading this Chapter, *God is about to break your silence!*

Nabal and his entire camp were under a death sentence; David and his men had planned to kill them because Nabal declined David's request.

Her Silent Warfare

1 Samuel 25:10-12

10 And Nabal answered David's servants, and said, **Who is David?** and who is the son of Jesse? there be many servants now a days that break away every man from his master.
11 Shall I then take my bread, and my water, and my flesh that I have killed for my shearers, and give it unto men, whom I know not whence they be?
12 So David's young men turned their way, and went again, and came and told him all those sayings.

Innocent blood was about to be shed because of Nabal's wickedness, but God used the voice of Abigail to save her family and the entire camp. Abigail began to move in wisdom. She knew that she could not consult her husband concerning her actions because he didn't have good judgement. As a matter of fact, he was a fool! The name Nabal literally means *fool* or *senseless*. Abigail moved in secret and in silence to secure the victory. I shared previously that knowing *when* to speak is just as important as *what* you speak. If she had gone to Nabal with her concerns, death would not have been prevented because Nabal would not have taken heed to her words; to him Abigails words were worthless.

Consider Abigail's actions. When Abigail opened up her mouth, her words were seasoned with wisdom and she operated in divine timing. This is why her voice reversed the sentence of death from of her house. The devil doesn't want you to open your mouth because when you do every curse assigned to destroy you and your family will be reversed.

Abigail's action delivered her entire family and the entire camp. There are a few insights that I've gleaned from Abigail that will provide a pattern for those who have found themselves in similar situations and have been settling for remaining silent instead of using their voice for victory.

Abigail knew who she was married to, she knew that Nabal would not hear her or take heed to her voice so she had to trust her instincts when she felt the need to intervene. Also, Abigail had to pick the right timing to discuss her actions. And even though Nabal was still upset, Abigail's actions saved so many lives.

1 Samuel 25:36-38

36 And Abigail came to Nabal; and, behold, he held a feast in his house, like the feast of a king; and Nabal's heart was merry within him, for he was very drunken: wherefore **she told him nothing**, less or more, until the morning light.
37 But it came to pass in the morning, when the wine was gone out of Nabal, and his wife had **told**

him these things, that his heart died within him, and he became as a stone.
38 And it came to pass about ten days after, that the Lord smote Nabal, that he died.

It's my prayer that you never again downplay the value of your voice. You have an anointing to get victory for your entire family. Right now, I break the silence and I activate your voice. The mantle of Abigail rests on you now, in the name of Jesus! Amen.

CHAPTER 5

Her Warfare of Regret

There will always be someone willing to hurt you, put you down, gossip about you, belittle your accomplishments and judge your soul. It is a fact that we all must face. However, if you realize that God is a best friend that stands beside you when others cast stones you will never be afraid, never feel worthless and never feel alone.
~Shannon Alder

Common sense is one of the most unused commodities available to man.
~Craig D. Lounsbrough

Don't kill yourself just because you think and feel you are empty. God needs empty vessels to fill!
~Ernest Agyemang Yeboah

Her Warfare of Regret

There is no such thing as a life without regrets. Regret is both a feeling and a pattern of thinking where one dwells on or constantly replays and thinks about an event, reactions, or other actions that could have been taken. Regret can become a painful burden that interferes with your present happiness, causes you grief, and restricts your future. Regret is a powerful anchor that will hold us firmly in the past and prevent us from enjoying the present. It is an all-consuming stronghold that will interject its destructive presence into the happiest of moments, pulling a dark cloud over a life that has managed to find a sense of peace.

If we have lived very long at all, there is a pretty good chance we have done at least a few things we wish we hadn't. We live daily with the Warfare of Regret because there are some things that though we wish we could go back and undo, we can't.

This is the reality of Sarai in Genesis 16:2. It's obvious that God gave Abraham a prophetic glimpse of his future, showing him that he would become the father of many nations, yet Sarai was on another page. Sarai viewed God's promise to her husband as an impossibility and she felt that God had waited too long. Sarai doubted and in one passage she laughed! Sarai was so far removed from having a baby that she recommended a remedy that she would later regret.

In Genesis 16:2, we read, "And Sarai said unto Abram, 'Behold now, the Lord hath restrained me from bearing: I pray thee, go in unto my maid; it may be that I may obtain children by her.' And Abram hearkened to the voice of Sarai."

So many of us are just like Sarai. Whenever God speaks to us and says something beyond our ability to comprehend, we, like Sarai, start to manipulate our circumstances to produce our own miracle. This put Abraham in a position where Sarai's doubt created an environment of disobedience. Although God's plan was to produce through Sarah, Abraham complied with her request and through Hagar, Abraham fathered Ishmael which brought him grief.

Genesis 21:9-11 tells us that, "And Sarah saw the son of Hagar the Egyptian, which she had born unto Abraham, mocking. Wherefore she said unto Abraham, Cast out this bondwoman and her son: for the son of this bondwoman shall not be heir with my son, even with Isaac. And the thing was very grievous in Abraham's sight because of his son."

"Emotional remedies can open the gate to a lifetime of regret." ~**Apostle Lizelle Bradley**

As women we will all agree that we have all made some decisions out of desperation and these decisions have put us in some dysfunctional positions. Even though God gave us the grace to recover and we now see the fulfillment of **Romans 8:28** in our lives we still at times regret dating or even marrying a certain person, having a child from a particular person, and those who have battled with drug abuse or alcohol abuse have also likely lived in a place of regret. Many women, as you read this book, are reminded of decisions you have made that have caused you to live in regret.

Sarai was living in her place of promise; the word of the Lord has been fulfilled in her life. But there's one problem, Sarai was warring with regret!

It's painful to coexist with stuff you can't change!
~Apostle Lizelle Bradley

Hagar and her son had to go! The level of bitterness Sarai felt towards Hagar and Isaac was birthed out of a decision that she made, only to later regret. You will be surprised by the number of women who are walking in bitterness, regret, resentment, anger, remorse, and hate because they cannot shake loose from the shackles of a bad decision.

If your decision was not a blessing, you must see it as a lesson. ~Apostle Lizelle Bradley

God revealed to me some remedies for the regret that so many women are shackled by. I want you to take each insight to heart, the first thing the Lord simply said to me is listed below.

1. **Make necessary adjustments for the things you cannot change.**
   Since there are some things that have transpired in our lives that you simply cannot change, you have to change the way you see it; change the way you respond to it; change how much you think about it; and change how much you talk about it.

   You must choose to see the lessons learned and the wisdom that's been gained.

2. **Forgive yourself.**
   Don't continue to penalize yourself because of something in your past. Release, Refocus and Rebound!

---

*There's more to your life than the mistakes you've made! ~**Apostle Lizelle Bradley***

---

3. **Be prayerful and sensitive to God in future decisions.**
   You must trust that God has a plan for your life and that He knows what's best for you. If that's the case, then you will never make another decision without conversing with Him. "In all

your ways acknowledge Him and He will direct your path," as we read in Proverbs 3:6.

This is the only way you and I will live a life without regrets.

CHAPTER 6

The Warfare of Her Rejection

God never said that the journey would be easy, but He did say that the arrival would be worthwhile
~Max Lucado

God's work done in God's way will never lack God's supplies ~Hudson Taylor

---

God will meet you where you are in order to take you where He wants you to go
~Tony Evans

The Warfare of Her Rejection

"The biggest hurdle is rejection. Any business you start, be ready for it. The difference between successful people and unsuccessful people is the successful people do all the things the unsuccessful people don't want to do. When 10 doors are slammed in your face, go to door number 11 enthusiastically, with a smile on your face."
John Paul DeJoria

Rejection is an almost unavoidable aspect of being human. No one has ever succeeded in love, ministry, business, or in life without first facing rejection. We all experience it, and yet, those times when we do are often the times we feel the most alone, outcast, and unwanted. In fact, so much of the hurt and struggle we endure isn't even based on the rejection itself but on what we tell ourselves about the experience, the cruel ways we put ourselves down, or flood ourselves with hopeless thoughts about the future.

While preparing for this chapter the Lord revealed some insights to me concerning the Warfare of Rejection. This is a chapter where I really want you to lean in and hear God for yourself because I firmly believe that the release you need to be free from rejection is about to hit your life.

---

*Rejection can change the way you see and respond to life. ~**Apostle Lizelle Bradley***

The Warfare of Her Rejection

In Genesis 29:16-17, we are introduced to Laban who had two daughters: the name of the elder was Leah, and the name of the younger was Rachel. Leah was tender eyed; but Rachel was beautiful and well favoured."

When you research the life of Leah you will discover the many layers of rejection she had to endure and overcome. Notice her description in the text, she was tender eyed. Which meant that Leah had a weak eye, this defect caused her to be familiar with whisper as she walked into a room. This, no doubt, had to impact her self-esteem and even self-worth. To add insult to injury, in the same verse it says "...*but* Rachel was beautiful and well favoured."

Her warfare is more than just physical but it is now mental because in her mind she was living with the comparison of her sister; she was devalued, depreciated, and diminished.

These are just a few adjectives that describe how Leah viewed herself. And the very moment she can be proud, she was rejected yet again. She had no idea that her father sought to manipulate his nephew by giving him Leah after he'd worked 7 years for Rachel. All Leah knew was that for the last few months she'd been preparing to get married. The day after her wedding, and after she and Jacob had consummated their marriage, she overheard a conversation between Jacob and her father. Jacob asked her father, "What is this?"

Genesis 29:25 Unveiled Version

25 The next morning Jacob looked and instead of Rachael it was Leah, He cried out to Laban, What is it? Did not I work for Rachel? How did I get stuck with Leah?

I need every reader to imagine the level of rejection Leah must have felt at this particular moment in her life. To finally have someone in her life that she thought would love her for who she was, she deals with rejection instead. Wow! This had to be a very low moment in the life of Leah because it's the very moment she discovered she was *still* unwanted!

So many have been hit with this same blow. Just when you thought you were finally over the feelings of rejection, you were hit with another blow.

Jacob agreed to work an additional seven years for the one he really wanted—Rachael. So, for seven years, Leah was in a marriage feeling unwanted. Can you see the demon of rejection at work in her life? Yet God is so faithful that He will always provide you with a way to break free.

The Warfare of Her Rejection

In Genesis 29:31, we read, "And when the Lord saw that Leah was hated, he opened her womb: but Rachel was barren."

When God opened up her womb, Leah thought that her Warfare with Rejection was over. She started producing from a painful place. She gave birth to gain her husband's attention, love, and acceptance. However, nothing she did made the pain of rejection go away until she got a revelation, *Despite the rejection I have faced in life, I need to focus on my relationship with God and I need to start rejoicing!*

That's your word, forget the fact that you have been rejected. I command you to drop this book, pick up your tambourine, and start rejoicing.

In Genesis 29:35, we are told, "And she conceived again, and bare a son: and she said, Now will I praise the Lord: therefore she called his name Judah; and left bearing."

I declare that the spirit of rejection will no longer have the victory. I declare that you are breaking free even now, and that you are free to rejoice.

In this very moment you are moving from rejection to rejoicing! You will no longer be haunted by the experiences of your past. You will walk into to your future with absolute confidence in an almighty God. In Jesus' name, Amen.

CHAPTER 7

The Warfare of Her Ministry

The family should be a closely knit group. The home should be a self-contained shelter of security; a kind of school where life's basic lessons are taught; and a kind of church where God is honored; a place where wholesome recreation and simple pleasures are enjoyed. ~Billy Graham

---

Each day of our lives we make deposits in the memory banks of others.
~Charles (Chuck) Swindoll

Whoever is spared personal pain must feel himself called to help in diminishing the pain of others. We must all carry our share of the misery which lies upon the world." ~Albert Schweitzer

---

"Worry does not empty tomorrow of its sorrows; it empties today of its strength." ~Corrie Ten Boom

The Warfare of Her Ministry

This is an amazing time and season for female leadership like never before. Women, and more so women of color, are rising to new heights in business, leadership, politics, and even ministry. There's a mantle released in this hour for women who have been hand-picked by God to do exploits in the earth. Think about this, God himself has not only graced you with a gift but He has chosen you for such a time as this to make an uncommon impact.

I really want every woman to know that there's an uncommon grace on your life. Lean into this chapter because I am extremely passionate about women in leadership, and especially women in ministry. I have seen and experienced first-hand the warfare we face when we decide to do what God has called us to do.

My yes got me in this!!!!
Apostle Lizelle Bradley

Saying 'Yes!' to God's call on your life is met with challenges like you would not believe. You would think that because you said yes, that God would protect you from jealousy, envy, strife, sabotage, lies, and rumors, but I'm discovering that these attacks come with the anointing.

If you show me someone who's anointed, I will show you someone who knows what it is to be attacked, afflicted, and even assaulted because the enemy fears who you are in God. And he does not want you to walk in your grace and your anointing.

Understand this: There are certain levels of warfare that you will never experience until you are in sync with the assignment God has attached to your life.

God began to reveal to me a principle that I'm reminded of every time the enemy shows up and it's simply, ***Warfare comes with the yes!***

I need every woman in ministry to hear me clearly, *The warfare you have experienced, are experiencing, and will experience is connected to the 'Yes!' that you gave to God!* This is why you must be confident in your call. Don't allow the enemy to talk you out of what God has called you to do.

I'm reminded of a very powerful woman by the name of Deborah. The story of Deborah is in **Judges 4**, and the song is in **Judges 5.** Deborah judged Israel; judges were Israel's charismatic leaders in the days before the monarchy. These leaders usually acquired their political authority after they saved Israel through battle.

God used Deborah to not only bring a word but to release peace over the entire nation. It's amazing because Barak didn't have to listen to her, but when God places his anointing on your life, He will also give you a platform.

Barak understood that God's hand was on the life of Deborah. This distinction and grace released so much warfare against Deborah both privately and publicly. But the warfare she faced didn't make her weak, it pushed her to work even harder.

This is why I thank God for my husband, because when I heard the voice of God telling me to be affirmed as an Apostle so many didn't understand nor did they believe it was God. Yet God gave me a husband who I didn't have to convince. He supported me in the face of those who sought to downplay what God had called me to do and those sought to discourage *him* by making him feel I was moving out of the will of God.

Women, this is when you must be confident in what God said. You may not get the support you desire and you may even lose friends but you can't back up from what God called you to do. I witnessed people smiling in my face who didn't believe that I had heard from God. Some even showed up to the affirmation and yet doubted, but I knew what God said and my husband and ministry had my back. I couldn't go down with so many holding me up.

Let me help the many who are afraid to completely obey God, and those of you who fear who you will lose or what you will lose. The warfare comes with the call to qualify those that are called! Don't you ever forget that!

I release now the Mantle of Deborah upon every woman reading this book. I pray for the Spirit of Boldness to hit you like never before and like Deborah, I pray you arise and that you walk in the anointing that God has released on your life.

You may be the weaker vessel but you are anointed to carry weight! ~***Apostle Lizelle Bradley***

CHAPTER 8

The Warfare of Her Family

Faith is not only daring to believe, it is also daring to act. When I believe in myself as a son of God, I attribute to all men the same quality. This goes for men of every class, creed and color. The proof that I believe this way will be measured by the way I act towards others. ~Wilfred Peterson

Every day you need to get a full dose of the Word and mediate on scripture, and if you discipline yourself and remain consistent, your faith will grow and mature, and remember that God, the Word, and your faith, is a recipe for success.
~Stephanie Williams

Hearing how God is moving in other places encourages and inspires our faith for what God wants to do in our own corner of the world.
~Matt Brown

The Warfare of Her Family

There are three realities that will cause most women to engage in constant warfare. The moment I mention these three things, if you are a woman you will no doubt identify with at least one of them that has caused you to go to war. They are:

- Family
- Friends
- Feelings

I want to really focus on the warfare we face with our families. As women of God, women in ministry, and as women in general we carry our families very close to our hearts. If you really want to see the best in us... and the worst in us involve our families.

We sacrifice and suffer so that our families can excel. We give unselfishly so that our families can have it better than we had it. But it's a hurtful thing when we are mishandled, mistreated, betrayed, lied on, used, and abused by our families.

When these experiences occur, we must be sensitive to the activity of the enemy because sometimes the enemy will use family to pull us out of the will of God. You will be surprised by those who are too stressed, depressed and overwhelmed to do anything for God. Some have been so hurt by those they've tried to help that they no longer have the same passion to be a blessing.

The Warfare of Her Family

It's warfare when the very ones you help turn on you! **Apostle Lizelle Bradley**

Some of the most devastating feelings are when one is not able to trust, depend on and confide in your own family. With some of them, the only time you hear from them is when they need you, or if they start to get close it's only because they are seeking to use you.

Whenever you notice these signs please know that you can still love your family without allowing them to misuse you. As a matter of fact, you can still fulfill your assignment in their lives without permitting them to get over on you. If you are honest, you will admit that some of them just aren't right and they are not trying to get right; you must use wisdom so that you don't become weary. Carrying them will make you weary; fighting for them will make you weary; always being there for them will make you weary; and taking on their responsibilities will no doubt make you weary. So, as you war for your family I pray for divine wisdom to be your portion so that you can fulfill your assignment without becoming overwhelmed and frustrated.

You must not forget that you have an assignment and it is to bring deliverance to your family, but the enemy wants you to be so hurt by them that you refuse to help them. You have the mantle of Esther and this mantle will cause your family to experience favor!

*"Then Queen Esther answered, 'King Xerxes, I hope you will show me your favor. I hope you will be pleased to let me live. That's what I want. **Please spare my people**. That's my appeal to you. My people and I have been sold to be destroyed. We've been sold to be killed and wiped out.'"*

Esther 7:3-4a

You have an anointing to stop the enemy right in his tracks and to reverse the curse off of your family! Like Esther, you have been handpicked by God as a deliverer for your family. When you pray, they will be delivered, healed, released from prison, set free from addictions, and rescued from death. **So, the enemy desires for you to be in war *with* them and not war *for* them!** But the devil is a liar! I declare that you will walk in Esther's anointing and that your family will experience God's grace like never before!

How do you guard your spirit from becoming polluted by people in your family?

1. **Identify the activity of the enemy at work through them.**
   In Ephesians 6:12, we learn "For we wrestle not

against flesh and blood, but against principalities, against powers, against the rulers of the darkness of this world, against spiritual wickedness in high places. Know that the enemy will use them to stop you if you let him.

2. **Pray and ask God for strategy and solutions.**
   Matthew 5:9 states, "Blessed *are* the peacemakers: for they shall be called the children of God." Know that in every situation, you are anointed for peace. Make sure you're not a part of the problem, but the solution.

3. **Obey the instructions God gives you.**
   Please know that a part of being a spirit-filled believer is being forgiving, long-suffering, forbearing, and patient, just to name a few. Sometimes God won't allow us to just dismiss them or cut them off, because when we forgive, when we suffer long with them, and when we are patient with them, they get a revelation of the God we serve. So, this calls for sensitivity to God and absolute obedience to his instructions. You're anointed for this!

CHAPTER 9

The Warfare of Her Faith

Jesus took the tree of death so you could have the tree of life. ~Tim Keller

---

The work of redemption was accomplished by Christ in His death on the cross and has in view the payment of the price demanded by a holy God for the deliverance of the believer from the bondage and burden of sin. In redemption the sinner is set free from his condemnation and slavery to sin.
~John F. Walvoord

Your talent is God's gift to you. What you do with it is your gift back to God. ~Leo Buscaglia

The Warfare of Her Faith

I want to look at a passage with timeless revelation and insight, and I sincerely believe that so many will be blessed and challenged as we look at the life of this woman with an issue of blood and the warfare she faced while walking by faith.

Matthew 9:20-22 states, "And, behold, a woman, which was diseased with an issue of blood twelve years, came behind him, and touched the hem of his garment: For she said within herself, If I may but touch his garment, I shall be whole. But Jesus turned him about, and when he saw her, he said, Daughter, be of good comfort; thy faith hath made thee whole. And the woman was made whole from that hour."

Allow me to say that even though our circumstance or situation may be different from this woman in our text, I believe that all of us know exactly what it feels like to be in a faith fight!

As women, we are always in warfare with our faith, as I stated in a previous chapter—even though we are the weaker vessels we were built to carry the heavier weights. Now, that's not always *physical* weight. Sometimes we have to carry our man, our children, our grandchildren, our family, our business, our ministry, or simply the heavy loads of life. Whenever life puts us in these positions, we must fight with our faith.

The Warfare of Her Faith

When faith becomes mandatory, the enemy will fight against you like never before so that you give up on **your** assignment. I often wondered why God allows the enemy so much access to us, our family, our marriage, our children, our finances, and the list goes on and on. But one day I got the revelation that sometimes God will permit the fight to strengthen our faith! As a matter of fact, what you're fighting is all about your faith!

Your warfare is over your faith, it attempts to change your connection to God; your obedience to the Word of God; your commitment to the work of God; and your conversations about God. Yes; your warfare is about your faith.

This woman in the text was in a war! She was fighting to be healed. She was fighting to be whole, but she had to fight using her faith because her efforts outside of faith were fruitless! Mark 5:26 says, "And had suffered many things of many physicians, and had spent all that she had, and was nothing bettered, but rather grew worse."

Her money could not get her healed! Her doctor could not make her whole! Her friends could not cure her! She had to fight with her Faith. Have you ever been **where your** faith was the only weapon you had left?

The Warfare of Her Faith

Just about two years ago I had a very interesting incident to happen to me. I went in for a simple medical procedure. Only to return some days later with my doctor saying that he needed to speak with me. He expressed to me that while he was performing the procedure, he noticed some fibroid tumors. They had gotten so big that they had trapped some cancer cells against the wall of my uterus preventing them from spreading. I never knew that I had any of this going on in my body, but my faith was already working.

This is why your faith should always be at work. When faith becomes your lifestyle problems will arise, sickness may attack, agendas sent from the pit of hell designed to kill, steal, and destroy will never prosper because your faith will go before you and pulverize the enemy's plan. Now here's the shout...Often, by the time you find out how bad your situation was, your faith will have already secured the victory for you.

In other words, my faith was in warfare for a healing that I didn't even know I needed; my faith had secured my victory before I was informed that I was facing a battle. Let me speak this over your life right now, because you have decided to walk by faith and not by sight:

The Warfare of Her Faith

- Your faith is fighting right now for a financial release that you don't even know you need!

- Your faith is blocking the daggers and darts thrown at you by the enemy that you never even saw coming.

- Your faith is setting up situations to turn your sons and daughters in God's direction. You're going to look up and they will be sitting right behind you in Church.

---

*When faith becomes your only option, then you're ready for a miracle! ~**Apostle Lizelle Bradley***

Allow me to share these principles:

1. Never take on any problem by yourself; you can not do it without faith.

2. Whenever you begin to feel defeated use the Word to strengthen your faith; faith comes by hearing.

3. Whenever you feel overwhelmed, overlooked, overworked. Press into his presence; it's in his presence that faith is **recognized** and **rewarded**.

The Warfare of Her Faith

The woman in the text got into the presence of Jesus and released her faith and the Lord healed her on the spot! Her issue dried up.

We read in Matthew 9:21, "For she said within herself, If I may but touch his garment, I shall be whole."

I declare that as you walk by faith that every issue assigned to destroy you is being dismantled.

- Physical issues will dry up!
- Financial issues will dry up!
- Marital issues will dry up!
- Business issues will dry up!
- Spiritual issues will dry up!

I decree that your faith will make you whole and that you will live in total victory, in Jesus' name.

CHAPTER 10

The Warfare of Her Deliverance

Truth is inseparable from the illusory belief that from the figures of the unreal one day, in spite of all, real deliverance will come.
~Theodor W. Adorno

God will lead you into a deliverance where the means that delivers you will be those who would destroy you. ~Edwin Louis Cole

God wants you to be delivered from what you have done and from what has been done to you - Both are equally important to Him. ~Joyce Meyer

I want to look at an episode from Rahab's life, that in my estimation reveals her desire to be delivered. Despite her reputation as a prostitute, I believe that her real testimony was that she was a survivor. Rahab displayed determination that led to her deliverance.

You can be delivered!
Apostle Lizelle Bradley

Yes, you can experience true deliverance, however it will require your participation. You must take seriously your role in your deliverance. The one key role that we all play in our deliverance is simply our decisions.

Our decisions must reflect our desire to be delivered. ~***Apostle Lizelle Bradley***

Deliverance is defined as the act of being rescued or set free.

So many have experienced being rescued or even set free, but after they were delivered, they began to make decisions that were counter to their desire for deliverance, so they find themselves ensnared again.

"As a dog returneth to his vomit, so a fool returneth to his folly" Proverbs 26:11

The Warfare of Her Deliverance

This is why I say Rahab represented someone who really desired deliverance; her decisions were clear and calculated.

In Joshua 2:9-14 states, "And she said unto the men, I know that the Lord hath given you the land, and that your terror is fallen upon us, and that all the inhabitants of the land faint because of you. For we have heard how the Lord dried up the water of the Red sea for you, when ye came out of Egypt; and what ye did unto the two kings of the Amorites, that were on the other side Jordan, Sihon and Og, whom ye utterly destroyed. And as soon as we had heard these things, our hearts did melt, neither did there remain any more courage in any man, because of you: for the Lord your God, he is God in heaven above, and in earth beneath. **Now therefore, I pray you, swear unto me by the Lord, since I have shewed you kindness, that ye will also shew kindness unto my father's house, and give me a true token: And that ye will save alive my father, and my mother, and my brethren, and my sisters, and all that they have, and deliver our lives from death.** And the men answered her, Our life for yours, if ye utter not this our business. And it shall be, when the Lord hath given us the land, that we will deal kindly and truly with thee."

Rahab was in position to ask for whatever she wanted, but I firmly believe that God was already dealing with Rahab. She had already heard

The Warfare of Her Deliverance

about the greatness of God. And this was her moment to break free. See, sometimes it's hard to break free when you are benefiting. Rahab was making good money but it wasn't enough to stop her from being free.

So many reading this book right now are warring with:

- **Letting go**
- **Walking away**
- **Being free**
- **True deliverance**
- **Giving it up**

I certainly understand the struggle of being at war, but true deliverance will cost you something! You will not be able to live with the benefits and break free at the same time, you must be willing to experience total freedom. When God gave Rahab a divine opportunity to be free, she was willing to give up her past and press into her future.

Rahab's Revelation

Rahab no doubt had a revelation that she was the key holder to her family's deliverance, and so she seized the moment.

The Warfare of Her Deliverance

Rahab requested that the spies not only deliver her, but that they deliver everyone in her family.

Let me speak this prophetic word right now, *You are anointed to get deliverance for your entire family, this is why the enemy have sought to keep you ensnared but while you're reading this chapter the Lord himself is setting up a divine opportunity for your deliverance! I declare that no demon sent from the pit of hell to hinder your deliverance will prevail against you.*

Here are three helpful insights when the enemy seeks to hinder your deliverance.

1. **You must have a made-up mind.**
   You cannot allow the enemy to cause you to waver in your decision to be delivered. "A double minded man is unstable in all his ways," James 1:8

2. **You must be willing to go against the odds.**
   Things will not always be favorable when you're seeking to be free, but you must be determined to be delivered. "Cast not away therefore your confidence," Hebrew 10:35a

3. **You must respect the process.**
   Your deliverance may not happen overnight, so you cannot give up because you don't see all that you've asked God for. Know that deliverance in most cases takes time. "Being confident of this very thing, that he which hath begun a good work in you will perform *it* until the day of Jesus Christ," Philippians 1:6

   If God started it, He's faithful to finish it!
   Apostle Lizelle Bradley

AFTERWORD

1. You are loved by God!

   As a woman that God created, you are prized and cherished. You are adored. You are loved beyond measure. You are cared about deeply, delighted in, and treasured. And on top of all that, God likes you too!

2. You have unique abilities and a distinct purpose designed by God.

   God created you in His own image. You are a masterpiece, designed by the most skilled artisan the world has ever known.
   (ref. Psalm 139:14)

   When He created you, God chose specific talents, skills, and abilities for you. He had a specific purpose in mind for you and knew exactly who you needed to be to fulfill that purpose. No mistakes!

   You are a unique, on-purpose creation, designed to glorify God. *(ref. Ephesians 2:10)*

3. Your voice matters!

    You have opinions and ideas that are valuable. You're worth listening to, and your input and creativity make a difference!

    No matter where you've come from, who you've been, or what you've done, your story is valuable; share your story!

    Use your voice to honor God.

4. We need your strengths!

    The healthy church knows that God created male and female on purpose. God knew that the world—and churches and families and communities—would work best when both genders utilize their strengths.

    The church needs women to be women—not doormats, nosey gossips, or authority hogs—but the authentic, emotional, compassionate, strong beings that you are as God designed.

5. You are valuable!

    I have been to churches where the women's role was to sit quietly and let the men do the talking, deciding, and guiding. Sometimes this can send

The Warfare of A Woman

a harmful message. You are not second class, less than, or inept because you're not a man. There is more for you than to sit in quiet submission. You are valuable to God and to His church.

6. You are an indispensable part of the Body of Christ.

    Paul reminds us that every single believer has a unique place and function in the Body of Christ. That means you too, women!

    Maybe you don't pastor or usher, but you are important to the body of believers. The strong church thanks its women and realizes that without you and your unique function in this body, we wouldn't thrive nearly as well or be half as strong.

7. You are a delight, not a danger, or an annoyance.

    One church I know of refused to allow the women to have any scheduled gatherings because they were afraid it would turn into a gossip fest.

    While women are wise to guard against gossip, that church was sending a harmful message. Probably because of past experience or problems with a few women, the church was fearful of all women behaving unhealthily. However, women need to be treated as individuals, as a delight and not as a petty annoyance, or an afterthought.

8. You are cared about and loved as sisters in Christ.

   Women are essential to creating strong communities. You often have a knack for bringing people together, meeting needs, and loving on people well.

   As such, you need to be cared for and loved on by those in your life; to be told often how much you are appreciated and cared about; and to be treated as beloved sisters in Christ.

9. Any "not enough" is more than enough in Christ.

   One of the biggest epidemics in Christianity today is the epidemic of "not enough." With all of the pressures and expectations on women, many of you struggle with feelings of inadequacy or of being overworked.

The church needs to remind women that any "not enough" is more than enough in Christ. Jesus is your strength and help and the only One who can dispel the "not enough" for good. Because with Jesus you are always more than enough. *(ref. 2 Corinthians 9:8)*

CLOSING PRAYER

I prophetically speak over every reader of my book; that you not just read it but live it. I pray that even now your challenges in Warfare have already been minimized in your spirit. I DECREE and DECLARE that VICTORY has already been won; that your choices have already changed and you have begun to operate in boldness to defeat the Enemy. I prophesy that when this book hits the market, there will be a tangible anointing that shall cause a rendezvous of favour. I prophesy that as people walk past it on the shelves of bookstores, and as they see it on TV, they shall be drawn to its anointing which will cause an immediate impact on their lives.

In Jesus' name, Amen.

THE WARFARE OF A *Woman*
APOSTOLIC INSTRUCTIONS FOR *Victory*

JOURNAL

Warfare Journal

Warfare Journal

Warfare Journal

Warfare Journal

Warfare Journal

Warfare Journal

Warfare Journal

Warfare Journal

Warfare Journal

Warfare Journal

Warfare Journal

Warfare Journal

Warfare Journal

Warfare Journal

Warfare Journal

www.ingramcontent.com/pod-product-compliance
Lightning Source LLC
Chambersburg PA
CBHW052159110526
44591CB00012B/2003